English

Picture Dictionary

English
Picture Dictionary

Berlitz Publishing/APA Publications GmbH & Co. Verlag KG
Singapore Branch, Singapore

Contacting the Editors
Every effort has been made to provide accurate information in this
publication, but changes are inevitable. The publisher cannot be responsible
for any resulting loss, inconvenience or injury. We would appreciate it if
readers would call our attention to any errors or outdated information by
contacting Berlitz Publishing, 95 Progress Street, Union, NJ 07083, USA.
Fax: 1-908-206-1103, email: comments@berlitzbooks.com

Cover illustration by Chris L. Demarest
Interior illustrations by Chris L. Demarest (pages 3, 5, 7-9, 12-23, 26-43,
46-51, 54-67, 70-75, 78-85, 88-107, and 110-119)
Anna DiVito (pages 24, 25, 52, 53, 76, 77, 86, 87, and 120-123)
Claude Martinot (pages 10, 11, 44, 45, 68, 69, 108, and 109)

Printed in Singapore by Insight Print Services (Pte) Ltd., December 2004

Dear Parents,

The Berlitz Kids™ *Picture Dictionary* will create hours of fun and productive learning for you and your child. Children love sharing books with adults, and reading together is a natural way for your child to develop language skills in an enjoyable and entertaining way.

In 1878, Professor Maximilian Berlitz had a revolutionary idea about making language learning accessible and fun. These same principles are still successfully at work today. Now, more than a century later, research shows that children learn their first language just like they learn a foreign language—through instruction and interaction with teachers, parents or caregivers. Berlitz Kids™ combines the time-honored traditions of Professor Berlitz with this current research to create superior products that truly help children learn any language.

Berlitz Kids™ materials let your child gain access to language in a positive way. The content and vocabulary in this book have been carefully chosen by language experts to provide basic words and phrases that form the foundation of a core vocabulary. In addition, the book will delight your child, since each word is used in an amusing sentence, and then illustrated in an engaging style. The pictures are a great way to capture your child's attention!

You will notice that most words are listed as separate entries. Every so often, though, there is a special page that shows words grouped together by theme. For example, if your child is especially interested in animals, he or she will find a special Animals page with lots of words and pictures grouped there. In addition, to help your child with phrases used in basic conversation, you and your child may want to look at the back of the book, where phrases about such things as meeting new people and a family dinner can be found.

The Berlitz Kids™ *Picture Dictionary* has an easy-to-use index at the back of the book. This index lists the words in alphabetical order, and gives the page number where the word appears in the main part of the book.

We hope the Berlitz Kids™ *Picture Dictionary* will provide you and your child with hours of enjoyable learning.

The Editors at Berlitz Kids™

a/an

A sandwich and an apple are the cat's lunch.

across

The fork is across from the spoon.

add

I like to add numbers.

adventure

What an adventure!

afraid

The elephant is afraid.

after

She eats an apple after lunch.

again and again

She jumps again and again.

agree

They need to agree.

air

A balloon is full of air.

airplane

See Transportation (page 108).

airport

Airplanes land
at an airport.

all

All the frogs
are green.

alligator

See Animals (page 10).

almost

He can
almost
reach it.

along

There are birds
along the path.

already

He already
has a hat.

and

I have two
sisters and two
brothers.

answer

Who wants to
answer the
teacher's
question?

ant

See Insects (page 52).

apartment

He is in the
apartment.

apple

The apple
is falling.

April

The month after
March is April.

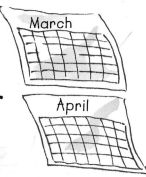

arm

See People (page 76).

armadillo

Some
armadillos
live in Mexico.

around

Someone is walking
around the stool.

art

Is it art?

as

He is as tall as
a tree!

Animals

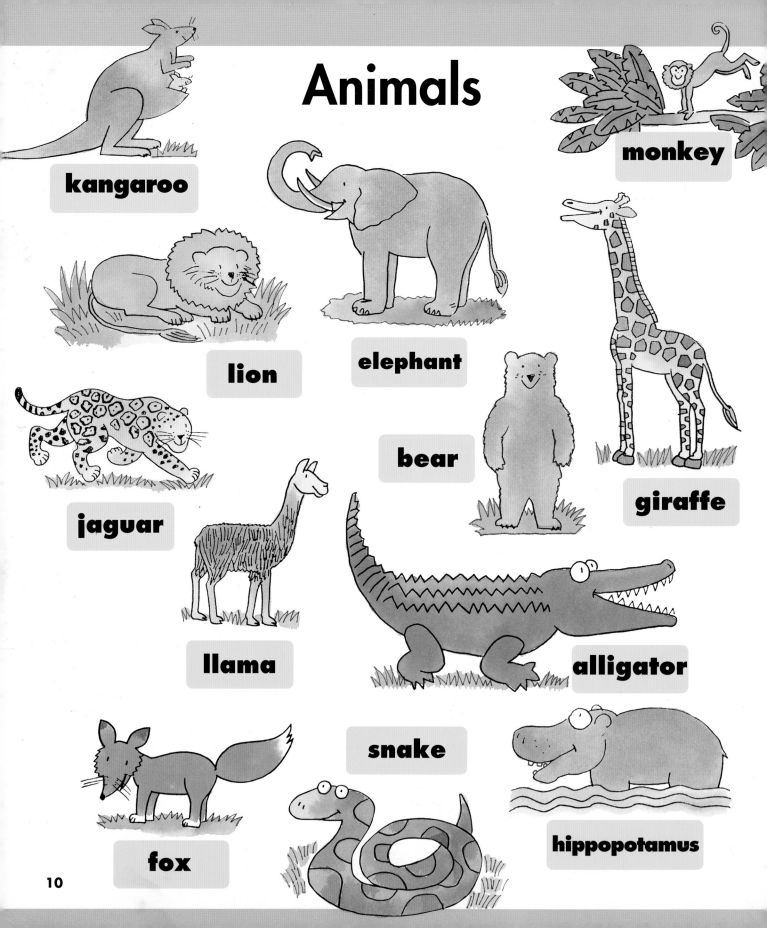

kangaroo

monkey

lion

elephant

bear

giraffe

jaguar

llama

alligator

fox

snake

hippopotamus

cow

horse

rooster

rabbit

goat

sheep

chicken

fish

pig

duck

frog

ask

It is time to ask, "Where are my sheep?"

aunt

My aunt is my mom's sister.

at

The cat is at home.

awake

The duck is awake.

attic

See Rooms in a House (page 86).

away

The cat is going away.

August

The month after July is August.

baby

The baby likes to eat bananas.

back

She is scratching his back.

bad

What a bad, bad monster!

bag

The bag is full.

bakery

Mmm! Everything at the bakery smells great!

ball

Can he catch the ball?

balloon

It is a balloon!

banana

The bananas are in the bowl.

band

The band plays loudly.

bandage

She has a bandage on her knee.

B

bank

Put your money
into the bank!

barber

The barber
cuts my hair.

bark

Dogs like to bark.

baseball

See Games and Sports (page 44).

basement

See Rooms in a House (page 86).

basket

What is in
the basket?

basketball

See Games and Sports (page 44).

bat

The bat is
sleeping.

bat

Hit the ball
with the
baseball bat!

bathe

She is bathing.

bathroom

See Rooms in a House (page 86).

be

Would you
like to be
my friend?

beach

I like to play at the beach.

beans

He likes to eat beans.

bear

See Animals (page 10).

beautiful

Look at the beautiful flowers!

because

She is wet because it is raining.

bed

The bed is next to the table.

bedroom

See Rooms in a House (page 86).

bee

See Insects (page 52).

beetle

See Insects (page 52).

before

Put on your socks before you put on your shoes.

begin

She begins to paint.

behind

The boy is behind the tree.

best

The red box is the best.

believe

This is too good to believe.

better

The belt is better than the pin.

bell

Don't ring that bell!

between

He is between two trees.

belt

See Clothing (page 24).

bicycle

See Transportation (page 108).

berry

Those berries look good.

big

He is very big.

biking

See Games and Sports (page 44).

bird

The bird is flying south for the winter.

birthday

She is one year old today. Happy birthday!

black

See Numbers and Colors (page 68).

blank

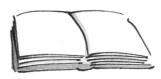

The pages are blank.

blanket

What is under that blanket?

blouse

See Clothing (page 24).

blow

The wind is starting to blow.

blue

See Numbers and Colors (page 68).

boat

See Transportation (page 108).

book

I am reading a book.

bookstore

You can buy a book at a bookstore.

boots

See Clothing (page 24).

bottle

The straw is in
the bottle.

bowl

Some food is still
in the bowl.

bowling

See Games and Sports (page 44).

box

Why is that fox
in the box?

boy

The boys are
brothers.

branch

Oh, no! Get
off that branch!

brave

What a brave
mouse!

bread

He likes bread
with jam and butter.

break

It is easy to
break an egg.

breakfast

Morning is the
time for breakfast.

bridge

The boat is under the bridge.

bring

She wants to bring the lamb to school.

broom

A broom is for sweeping.

brother

He is my brother.

brown

See Numbers and Colors (page 68).

brush

I need my brush.

bubble

The bathtub is full of bubbles.

bug

Do you know the name of this bug?

build

I want to build a box.

bus

See Transportation (page 108).

bush

There is a bird in the bush.

busy

He is very busy.

but

The pencil is on the table, but the book is on the chair.

butter

The bread and butter taste good.

butterfly

See Insects (page 52).

button

One button is missing.

buy

He wants to buy a banana.

by

She is standing by the cheese.

20

cage

The bird is on the cage.

cake

She likes to eat cake.

call

Remember to call me again.

camel

The camel is hot.

camera

Smile at the camera!

can

What is in that can?

candle

She is lighting the candle.

candy

Candy is sweet.

cap

See Clothing (page 24).

car

See Transportation (page 108).

card

I have five cards.

care

Her job is to care for pets.

carpenter

A carpenter makes things with wood.

carrot

A carrot is orange.

carry

Are you sure you want to carry that?

castanets

Click the castanets to the music!

castle

The king lives in a castle.

cat

The cat sees the mouse.

caterpillar

See Insects (page 52).

catch

He runs to catch the ball.

cave

Who lives in the cave?

celebrate

They are here to celebrate his birthday.

chair

He is sitting on a chair.

chalk

You can use chalk to write.

change

He wants to change his shirt.

cheer

It is fun to cheer for our team.

cheese

The mouse likes to eat cheese.

Clothing

vest

hat

raincoat

cap

earmuffs

shirt

tie

jacket

belt

pants

gloves

socks

sneakers

dress

coat

mittens

boots

scarf

blouse

sweater

skirt

shoes

shawl

cherry

He wants
a cherry.

chicken

See Animals (page 10).

child

She is a
happy child.

chocolate

He likes
chocolate.

circle

The robot is
drawing a circle.

circus

There are
clowns at
a circus.

city

This cow does
not live in
the city.

clap

He likes to
clap when he
is happy.

class

There is an
elephant
in my class.

classroom

A teacher works in a classroom.

clean (adjective)

The car is very clean.

clean (verb)

He is starting to clean his room.

climb

The bear likes to climb the tree.

clock

A clock tells time.

close (adverb)

The turtle is close to the rock.

close (verb)

He is going to close the window.

closet

See Rooms in a House (page 86).

cloud

The sun is behind the cloud.

clown
The clown is funny.

coat
See Clothing (page 24).

cold
It is cold in here!

comb (noun)
Where is
my comb?

comb (verb)
He likes to
comb his hair.

come
Come here!

computer
She is working
at her computer.

cook
It is fun to cook.

cookie
Mary wants
a cookie.

count
There are too
many stars
to count.

country

The country is beautiful.

cow

See Animals (page 10).

crayon

She is drawing with her crayons.

cricket

See Insects (page 52).

crowded

This elevator is crowded.

cry

Don't cry!

cup

He is drinking water from the cup.

cut

He cuts the carrots.

cute

She thinks her baby is cute.

dad

My dad and
I look alike.

dance

The pig likes
to dance and
play the drum.

danger

He is in danger.

dark

It is dark
at night.

day

The sun shines
during the day.

December

The month
after November
is December.

decide

It is hard
to decide.

decision

That is a good
decision.

deck

See Rooms in a House (page 86).

decorations

The decorations
look great!

deer

The deer is running in the woods.

dentist

The dentist has a big job.

department

This is the hat department.

desk

The desk is very messy.

different

The one in the middle is different.

difficult

This is difficult!

dig

A dog uses its paws to dig.

dining room

See Rooms in a House (page 86).

dinner

We eat dinner at six o'clock.

dinosaur

The dinosaur is having fun.

dirty

The pig is dirty.

dish

Do not drop the dishes!

do

He has a lot to do.

doctor

The doctor checks the baby.

dog

The dog has a funny hat.

doll

The doll is in the box.

dolphin

Dolphins live in the sea.

donkey

The donkey is sleeping.

door

What is behind the door?

down

The elevator is going down.

dragon

The dragon is cooking lunch.

draw

He likes to draw.

drawing

Look at my drawing!

dress

See Clothing (page 24).

drink

She likes to drink milk.

drive

He is too small to drive.

drop

He is going to drop the pie.

drum

He can play the drum.

dry

The shirt is dry.

duck

See Animals (page 10).

dust

There is dust under the bed.

E

each

Each snowflake is different.

ear

See People (page 76).

early

The sun comes up early.

earmuffs

See Clothing (page 24).

earn

We work to earn money.

east

The sun rises in the east.

eat

This bird likes to eat worms.

egg

The hen laid an egg.

eight

See Numbers and Colors (page 68).

eighteen

See Numbers and Colors (page 68).

eighty

See Numbers and Colors (page 68).

elephant

See Animals (page 10).

eleven

See Numbers and Colors (page 68).

empty

The bottle is empty.

end

It is time to end the game.

everything

Everything is purple.

enough

He has enough food!

everywhere

There are balls everywhere.

every

Every egg is broken.

excited

He is excited.

everyone

Everyone here has spots!

eye

See People (page 76).

F

face

See People (page 76).

factory

Cans are made
in this factory.

fall (verb)

He is about to fall.

fall (noun)

It is fall.

family

This is a big
family.

fan

Please turn off
the fan!

far

The moon is
far away.

faraway

She is going to
a faraway place.

fast

That train
is going fast!

fat

The pig is fat.

father

My father and I
look alike.

favorite

This is my
favorite toy.

feather

The feather is
tickling her nose.

February

The month
after January
is February.

feel

He likes to
feel safe.

fence

There is a zebra
on my fence.

fifteen

See Numbers and Colors (page 68).

fifty

See Numbers and Colors (page 68).

find

He is trying to
find his kite.

finger

See People (page 76).

fire

He can put
out the fire.

F

firefighter

The firefighter wears boots and a hat.

firefly

See Insects (page 52).

firehouse

Welcome to the firehouse!

first

The yellow one is first in line.

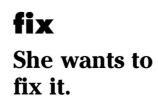

fish

See Animals (page 10).

five

See Numbers and Colors (page 68).

fix

She wants to fix it.

flag

She is waving a flag.

flat

The tire is flat.

flea

See Insects (page 52).

floor

There is a hole in the floor.

flower

The flower is growing.

flute

Robert plays the flute.

fly

See Insects (page 52).

fly

The bee wants to fly.

fog

He is walking in the fog.

food

He eats a lot of food.

foot

See People (page 76).

for

This is for you.

forget

He does not want to forget his lunch!

fork

He eats with a fork.

F

forty
See Numbers and Colors (page 68).

four
See Numbers and Colors (page 68).

fourteen
See Numbers and Colors (page 68).

fox
See Animals (page 10).

Friday
On Friday, we
go to the park.

friend
He is my
best friend.

frog
See Animals (page 10).

front
She sits in front
of him.

fruit
He loves to
eat fruit.

full
The cart is
full of lizards.

fun
She is having
fun.

funny
What a
funny face!

game

Checkers is a game we play in the park.

garage

See Rooms in a House (page 86).

garden

Roses are growing in the garden.

gate

The gate is open.

get

The mice are trying to get the cheese.

giraffe

See Animals (page 10).

girl

The girl is dancing.

give

I want to give you a present.

glad

She is glad to see you.

glass

Windows are made of glass.

glasses

This owl wears glasses.

gloves

See Clothing (page 24).

go

Go to your room!

goat

See Animals (page 10).

golf

See Games and Sports (page 44).

good

What a good dog!

good-bye

Good-bye!

goose

A goose is riding a bicycle.

gorilla

The gorilla is eating a banana.

grab

She wants to grab the bananas.

grandfather

I have fun with my grandfather.

grandma

Grandma is my dad's mother.

grandmother

My grandmother likes to bake.

grandpa

Grandpa is my mom's father.

grape

The mouse likes to eat grapes.

grass

Cows eat grass.

grasshopper

See Insects (page 52).

Games and Sports

baseball

basketball

golf

ping-pong

running

bowling

ice skating

soccer

skiing

tennis

biking

swimming

gray

See Numbers and Colors (page 68).

great

This is a great party.

green

See Numbers and Colors (page 68).

groceries

The groceries are falling out.

ground

They live in the ground.

group

This is a group of artists.

grow

He wants to grow.

guess

It is fun to guess what is inside.

guitar

My robot plays the guitar.

hair
See People (page 76).

half
Half the cookie is gone.

hall
See Rooms in a House (page 86).

hammer
Hit the nail with the hammer!

hammock
Dad is sleeping in the hammock.

hand
See People (page 76).

happy
This is a happy face.

hard
The rock is hard.

harp
She plays the harp very well.

hat
See Clothing (page 24).

have
Soon they will all have hats.

he
He is under the table.

head
See People (page 76).

hear
See People (page 76).

heart
The heart is red.

helicopter
See Transportation (page 108).

hello
Hello.
How are you?

help
I need help!

her/his
This is her tail.

here
I live here.

hi
Hi!

hide
She is too big
to hide under
the box.

high
The star is
high in the sky.

hill
She is coming
down the hill.

hippopotamus

See Animals (page 10).

hit

He hits the
ball.

hold

He has to hold her
hand now.

hole

He is digging
a hole.

hooray

We are winning!
Hooray!

hop

They know how
to hop.

horse

See Animals (page 10).

hospital

Doctors work at
the hospital.

hot

Fire is hot.

hotel

He is staying at
the hotel.

hour

In an hour, it is going to be two o'clock.

house

The house has many windows.

how

How does he do that?

hug

Give me a hug!

huge

That cat is huge!

hundred

See Numbers and Colors (page 68).

hungry

I think he is hungry.

hurry

She has to hurry.

hurt

It does not have to hurt.

husband

He is her husband.

I

"I am so cute!" she says.

ice

We skate on the ice.

ice cream

Clara likes ice cream.

idea

She has an idea.

important

He looks very important.

in

What is in that box?

inside

He is inside the house.

into

Do not go into that cave!

island

The goat is on an island.

Insects

butterfly

wasp

(praying) mantis

fly

flea

beetle

mosquito

caterpillar

grasshopper

moth

bee

termite

firefly

cricket

ant

53

J

jacket
See Clothing (page 24).

jaguar
See Animals (page 10).

jam
Do you think she likes bread and jam?

January
January is the first month of the year.

jar
Jam comes in a jar.

job
It is a big job.

juice
She is pouring a glass of orange juice.

July
The month after June is July.

jump
The animal loves to jump.

June
The month after May is June.

junk
No one can use this junk.

kangaroo
See Animals (page 10).

keep
He wants to
keep the dog.

key
Which key
opens the lock?

kick
He wants to
kick the ball.

kind (adjective)
She is kind to
animals.

kind (noun)
What kind of
animal is that?

king
The king is
having fun.

kiss
Would you
like to give the
monkey a kiss?

kitchen

See Rooms in a House (page 86).

knife

A knife can
cut things.

kite

Kites can fly
high.

knock

He starts to
knock on the
door.

kitten

A kitten is a
baby cat.

know

He wants to know
what it says.

knee

See People (page 76).

ladder

He climbs the ladder.

lake

He is drinking from the lake!

lamp

He has a lamp on his head.

lap

He sits on his grandma's lap.

last

The pink one is last in line.

late

It is late at night.

laugh

It is fun to laugh.

laundry room

See Rooms in a House (page 86).

lazy

He is so lazy.

leaf

The tree has one leaf.

leave

She does not
want to leave.

left

This is your
left hand.

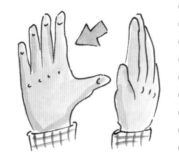

leg

See People (page 76).

lemon

She likes lemons.

leopard

One leopard is
losing its spots.

let

Papa is not going
to let him go.

letter

This letter is going
by airmail.

library

The library is
full of books.

lick

Lick the ice
cream before
it melts!

life

Life is
wonderful!

light

The sun gives us light.

lightning

Look! There's lightning!

like

He is going to like the cake.

like

She looks like a rock.

line

I can draw a line.

lion

See Animals (page 10).

listen

He does not want to listen to loud music.

little

The bug is little.

live

What a nice place to live!

living room

See Rooms in a House (page 86).

llama

See Animals (page 10).

lock

Do not forget to lock the door.

long

That is a long snake.

look

I use this to look at the stars.

lose

He does not want to lose his hat.

lost

Oh, no!
He is lost.

lots

There are lots of bubbles.

loud

The music is loud!

love (verb)

She is going to love the present.

love (noun)

Love is wonderful.

low

The bridge is low.

lunch

He eats nuts for lunch.

mad

The frogs are mad at each other.

man

The man is waving.

mail

The mail is here.

mango

Is he going to eat the whole mango?

mailbox

What is in that mailbox?

(praying) mantis

See Insects (page 52).

mail carrier

Our mail carrier brings us the mail.

many

There are too many dots!

make

A belt is easy to make.

map

The map shows where to go.

maraca
Shake those maracas!

March
The month after February is March.

math
He is not very good at math.

May
The month after April is May.

maybe
Maybe it is a ball.

mayor
The mayor leads the town.

me
Look at me!

mean
That has to mean "hello."

meat
I am eating meat, salad, and potatoes for dinner.

medicine
Take your medicine!

meet

It's a pleasure to meet you.

minute

It is one minute before noon.

meow

Cats say, "MEOW!"

mirror

He loves to look in the mirror.

mess

What a mess!

miss

He does not want to miss the airplane.

messy

The bear is a little messy.

mittens

See Clothing (page 24).

milk

He likes milk.

mix

Use the spoon to mix it.

mom

She is the baby's mom.

moon

The moon is up in the sky.

Monday

On Monday, we take baths.

more

She needs to buy more juice.

money

Look at all the money!

morning

The sun comes up in the morning.

monkey

See Animals (page 10).

mosquito

See Insects (page 52).

month

January and February are the first two months of the year.

most

Most of the milk is gone.

moth

See Insects (page 52).

mother

She is the baby's mother.

mountain

He is climbing up the mountain.

mouse

The mouse is skating.

mouth

See People (page 76).

move

They have to move.

movie

They are watching a movie.

Mr.

Say hello to Mr. Green.

Mrs.

Mrs. English is getting on the bus.

much

There is not much in the refrigerator.

music

They can play music.

my

This is my nose.

N

nail

Try to hit the nail!

name

His name begins with "R".

neck

See People (page 76).

necklace

She loves her necklace.

need

He is going to need a snack later.

neighbor

They are neighbors.

nest

The birds are near their nest.

never

She is never going to fly.

new

He has a new umbrella.

newspaper

Who cut my newspaper?

next (to)

She is next to
the rock.

next

The horse is
next.

nice

What a nice
clown!

night

It is dark at
night.

nine

See Numbers and Colors (page 68).

nineteen

See Numbers and Colors (page 68).

ninety

See Numbers and Colors (page 68).

no

No, you may
not go.

noise

He is making a
terrible noise.

noisy

They are
very noisy.

noon

It is noon.

Numbers and Colors

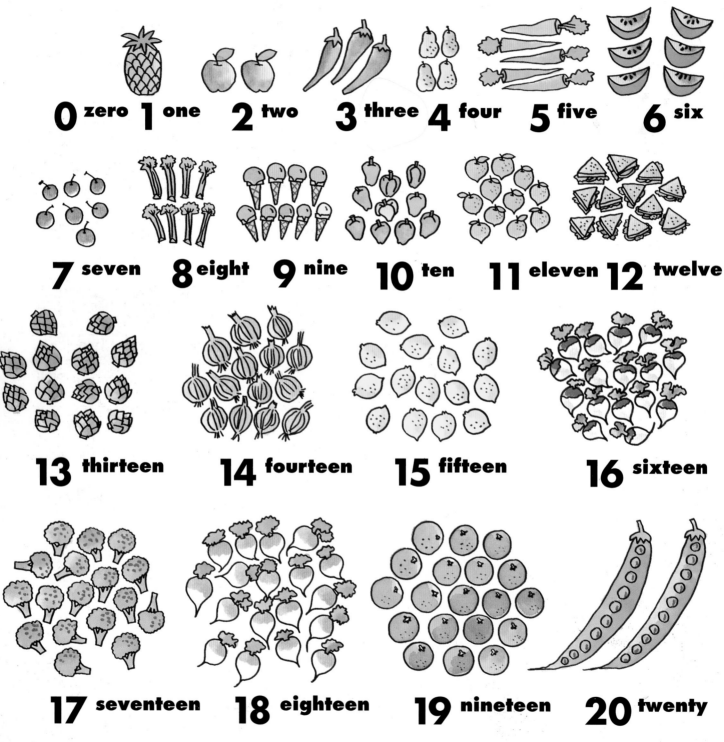

0 zero 1 one 2 two 3 three 4 four 5 five 6 six

7 seven 8 eight 9 nine 10 ten 11 eleven 12 twelve

13 thirteen 14 fourteen 15 fifteen 16 sixteen

17 seventeen 18 eighteen 19 nineteen 20 twenty

 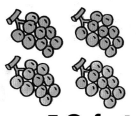  

30 thirty   **40** forty   **50** fifty   **60** sixty

70 seventy   **80** eighty   **90** ninety

100 one hundred   **1000** one thousand

Colors

black

blue

brown

gray

green

orange

pink

purple   yellow

red

tan

white

69

north

It is cold in the north.

nose

See People (page 76).

not

The bird is not red.

note

He is writing a note.

nothing

There is nothing in the bottle.

November

The month after October is November.

now

The mouse needs to run now.

number

There are five numbers.

nurse

She wants to be a nurse.

nut

I think he likes nuts.

ocean

This turtle swims in the ocean.

(one) o'clock

It is one o'clock.

October

The month after September is October.

of

The color of the airplane is yellow.

office

See Rooms in a House (page 86).

oh

Oh! What a surprise!

old

The alligator is very old.

on

The coat is on the chair.

once
Birthdays come
once a year.

one
See Numbers and Colors (page 68).

onion
He is chopping
an onion.

only
This is the
only food left.

open
The window
is open.

or
Do you want
the red one or
the blue one?

orange
See Numbers and Colors (page 68).

orange
He is squeezing
oranges.

ostrich
An ostrich can
run fast.

other
What is on the other side?

ouch
Ouch! That hurts!

out
He is going out of the house.

outdoors
We like to play outdoors.

oven
We bake cookies in the oven.

over
She is holding the umbrella over her head.

owl
The owl does not sleep at night.

own
He owns a book.

P

page

He is turning the page.

paint

The baby is sitting between the green and the blue paint.

painter

He is a painter.

pajamas

She is wearing pajamas to sleep.

pan

We cook in a pan.

panda

This panda is hungry.

pants

See Clothing (page 24).

See Clothing (page 24).

paper

Write on the paper!

parent

These parents have many babies.

park

We like to go to the park.

parrot

This parrot can say, "Cracker!"

part

A wheel is part of the car.

party

The ants are having a party.

pat

The baby tries to pat the dog.

paw

He wants to shake paws.

pea

He does not like to eat peas.

peach

Peaches grow on trees.

pen

The pen is leaking.

pencil

A pencil is used for drawing.

People •Your Body

head

face

stomach

knee

foot

leg

eye

thumb

hair

finger

neck

arm

hand

ear

tooth

see

nose

touch

mouth

smell

toe

hear

taste

77

penguin

There is a
penguin in
the sink.

pet

This pig is
a pet.

people

These people are
going up.

photograph

Look at the
photograph!

pepper

She is using too
much pepper.

piano

He plays the
piano very well.

peppers

Peppers are
tasty.

pick

This dog likes
to pick berries.

perfume

She is wearing
perfume.

picnic

They are having
a picnic.

picture

This is a picture of a rabbit.

pie

Who is eating the pie?

pig

See Animals (page 10).

pillow

You sleep with your head on a pillow

ping-pong

See Games and Sports (page 44).

pink

See Numbers and Colors (page 68).

pizza

We like to eat pizza.

place

The doctor places the glasses on his nose.

plan

It helps to plan ahead.

plant

He likes to plant nuts.

play

Do you want to play with us?

playground

Meet me at the
playground!

playroom

See Rooms in a House (page 86).

please

Please feed me!

pocket

What is in his
pocket?

point (noun)

It has a sharp point.
Ouch!

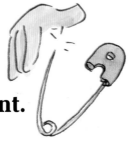

point (verb)

It is not polite
to point.

police officer

The police officer
helps us cross
the street.

police station

You can get
help at the
police station.

polite

He is so
polite!

pond

She falls into
the pond.

poor

This poor monkey does not have much money.

porch

See Rooms in a House (page 86).

post office

Letters go to the post office.

pot

It is time to stir the pot.

potato

These potatoes have eyes.

pound

Use a hammer to pound a nail.

present

Is the present for me?

pretty

It is not a pretty face.

prince

The prince is with his father.

princess

This princess has big feet.

prize
Look who wins
the prize.

purse
The purse
is full.

proud
She is proud of
her new hat.

push
He needs to
push hard.

pull
We're trying to
pull him up.

put
Don't put
your foot in
your mouth!

puppy
The puppy
is wet.

purple
See Numbers and Colors (page 68).

puzzle
Can you put the
puzzle together?

quack

"Quack, quack, quack!" sing the ducks.

quick

A rabbit is quick; a tortoise is slow.

quarrel

We do not like to quarrel.

quiet

Shh! Be quiet!

quarter

A quarter of the pie is gone.

quilt

Who is under the quilt?

quit

The raccoon wants to quit practicing.

queen

She is queen of the zebras.

quite

It is quite cold today.

question

She wants to ask a question.

R

rabbit
See Animals (page 10).

race
Who is going to win the race?

radio
They listen to the radio.

rain
She likes the rain.

rainbow
She is standing under a rainbow.

raincoat
See Clothing (page 24).

raindrop
Look at the raindrops.

raining
He is wet because it is raining.

read
Does he know how to read?

ready
The baby is not ready to go.

real

It is not a
real dog.

really

She is
really tall!

red

See Numbers and Colors (page 68).

refrigerator

We keep our
snowballs in the
refrigerator.

remember

It is hard to
remember his
phone number.

restaurant

She is eating at
a restaurant.

rice

Where is all
the rice?

rich

He is very
rich.

ride

It is fun to
ride a horse.

right

This is your
right hand.

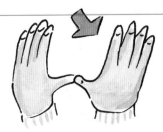

Rooms in a House

attic

deck

bedroom

bathroom

kitchen

dining room

garage

playroom

closet

bedroom

office

living room

hall

porch

basement

laundry room

R

ring (noun)

She has a new ring.

ring (verb)

The telephone is going to ring soon.

river

I am floating down the river.

road

The road goes over the hill.

robot

There's a robot in my window!

rock

This is a big rock!

roof

There is a cow on the roof.

room

The little house has little rooms.

rooster

See Animals (page 10).

root

The plant has deep roots.

rose

She likes roses.

round

These things are round.

rub

It is fun to rub his tummy.

rug

A bug is on the rug.

run

You need feet to run!

running

See Games and Sports (page 44).

S

sad

This is a sad face.

sailboat

See Transportation (page 108).

salad

He is making a salad.

salt

She is using too much salt.

same

They look the same.

sand

There is a lot of sand at the beach.

sandwich

It's a pickle sandwich! Yum!

sandy

The beach is sandy.

Saturday

On Saturday, we work together.

sausage

This dog likes sausages.

saw

A saw is for cutting.

say

She wants to say hello.

scarf

See Clothing (page 24).

school

He learns in school.

scissors

Look what he is cutting with the scissors.

scrub

He wants to scrub the tub.

sea

Whales live in the sea.

seat

The seat is too high.

secret

She is telling a secret.

see

See People (page 76).

seed

When you plant a seed, it grows.

sell

He has many balloons to sell.

send

Mom has to send a letter in the mail.

September

The month after August is September.

seven

See Numbers and Colors (page 68).

seventeen

See Numbers and Colors (page 68).

seventy

See Numbers and Colors (page 68).

shark

A shark has many teeth.

shawl

See Clothing (page 24).

she

She is hiding.

sheep

See Animals (page 10).

shirt

See Clothing (page 24).

shoes

See Clothing (page 24).

shop

He likes to shop.

short
He is too short.

shout
They have to shout.

shovel
She needs a bigger shovel.

show (noun)
They are in a show.

show (verb)
Open wide to show your new tooth!

shy
He is very shy.

sick
The rhinoceros is sick.

side
The tree is on the side of the house.

sidewalk
They are playing on the sidewalk.

sign
This is the bakery's sign.

silly

He has a silly smile.

sing

She loves to sing.

sister

They are sisters.

sit

They want to sit.

six

See Numbers and Colors (page 68).

sixteen

See Numbers and Colors (page 68).

sixty

See Numbers and Colors (page 68).

skateboard

See Transportation (page 108).

skates

See Transportation (page 108).

skating (ice)

See Games and Sports (page 44).

skiing

See Games and Sports (page 44).

skirt

See Clothing (page 24).

sky

The sky is full of stars.

sleep

He is ready to sleep.

slow

A rabbit is quick;
a tortoise is slow.

small

An ant is small.

smell

See People (page 76).

smile

What a big
smile!

smoke

Watch out for
the smoke!

snail

He has a snail
on his nose.

snake

See Animals (page 10).

sneakers

See Clothing (page 24).

snore

Try not to
snore.

snow

Snow is white
and cold.

snowball

He is throwing
snowballs.

so

She is so tall!

soap

He is using soap to wash.

soccer

See Games and Sports (page 44).

socks

See Clothing (page 24).

sofa

The zebras are sitting on the sofa.

some

Some of them are pink.

someday

Dad says I can drive . . . someday.

someone

Someone is behind the fence.

something

Something is under the rug.

song

What song do you think she is singing?

soon

Soon it is going to be noon.

sorry

She is sorry she dropped it.

soup

The soup is hot!

south

It is warm in the south.

special

This is a special car.

spider

This spider is friendly.

spoon

A spoon can't run; can it?

spring

Flowers grow in spring.

square

A square has four sides.

squirrel

There is a squirrel on that hat!

stamp

A stamp goes on a letter.

stand

She does not like to stand.

star

That star is winking.

start

They want to start with A.

stay

He has to stay inside.

step

Try not to step in the puddle.

stick

The dog wants the stick.

sticky

That candy is sticky.

stomach

See People (page 76).

stop

You have to stop for a red light.

store

She buys books at the store.

storm

She does not like the storm.

story

We all know this story.

strange

This is a strange animal.

strawberry

This strawberry is big!

street

There is an elephant in the street!

student

The students are all fish.

subway

See Transportation (page 108).

suddenly

Suddenly, it is raining.

suit

Something is spilling on his suit.

suitcase

What is in that suitcase?

summer

It is warm
in summer.

sun

The sun is hot.

Sunday

On Sunday,
we eat dinner
with grandma.

sunflower

The sunflower is
big and yellow.

sunny

She loves
sunny days.

sure

I am sure the
door is not going
to open.

surprised

She is
surprised.

sweater

See Clothing (page 24).

swim

The fish likes
to swim.

swimming

See Games and Sports (page 44).

table

There is a chicken on the table.

tail

He has a long tail.

take

He is going to take the suitcase with him.

talk

They like to talk on the phone.

tall

The red one is very tall.

tambourine

Shake that tambourine!

tan

See Numbers and Colors (page 68).

taste

See People (page 76).

taxi

See Transportation (page 108).

teacher

Our teacher helps us learn.

tear

She has a tear on her cheek.

telephone

People can call you on the telephone.

television

My goldfish likes to watch television.

tell

She tells him a story.

ten

See Numbers and Colors (page 68).

tennis

See Games and Sports (page 44).

tent

What is inside the tent?

termite

See Insects (page 52).

terrible

What a terrible mess!

thank

He wants to thank the firefighter.

that

What is that?

their

They are
pointing to
their suitcases.

these

No one wants
these eggs.

them

The shoes belong
to them.

they

See the mice?
They are dancing.

thin

One clown
is thin.

then

Get into bed.
Then sleep.

thing

What is this
thing?

there

There she is!

think

We use our brain to think.

thirsty

He is thirsty.

thirteen

See Numbers and Colors (page 68).

thirty

See Numbers and Colors (page 68).

this

This baby is sad.

those

Those babies are happy.

thousand

See Numbers and Colors (page 68).

three

See Numbers and Colors (page 68).

through

The ball is coming through the window.

throw

We like to throw the ball.

thumb

See People (page 76).

thunder

Thunder is loud.

Thursday

On Thursday, we wash clothes.

tie (noun)

See Clothing (page 24).

tie (verb)

Is he going to tie his shoelaces?

tiger

This is a tiger.

time

It is time to wash the dishes.

tire

One tire is flat.

tired

She is tired.

to

He is going to school.

today

Today is her birthday.

toe

See People (page 76).

together

They are sitting together.

tomato

Mmm! It is a big, juicy tomato.

tomorrow

Tomorrow is another day.

tonight

He is sleepy tonight.

too

The baby is singing, too.

tooth

See People (page 76).

toothbrush

My toothbrush is red.

top

The bird is on top.

touch

See People (page 76).

towel

He needs a towel.

town

The ant lives in a town.

toy

He has all kinds of toys.

track

That is a rabbit track.

train

See Transportation (page 108).

treat

A bone is a treat.

tree

There is a cow in that tree.

triangle

A triangle has three sides.

tricks

Her job is to do tricks.

trip (noun)

She is going on a trip.

trip (verb)

It is no fun to trip.

Transportation

airplane

train

van

skateboard

bicycle

skates

helicopter

sailboat

car

truck

boat

subway

horse

taxi

bus

109

truck

See Transportation (page 108).

trumpet

This is a trumpet.

try

He wants to try to climb it.

Tuesday

On Tuesday we wash the floors.

tulip

There is a tulip on his head.

turn

You have to turn the knob.

turtle

That is a fast turtle!

twelve

See Numbers and Colors (page 68).

twenty

See Numbers and Colors (page 68).

twins

They are twins.

two

See Numbers and Colors (page 68).

ugly

Do you think the toad is ugly?

up

It is scary up here!

umbrella

She has a yellow umbrella.

upon

The box is upon the box, upon the box.

uncle

My uncle is my dad's brother.

upside-down

He is upside-down.

under

There is something under the bed.

us

Come with us!

until

He eats until he is full.

use

He needs to use a comb.

V

vacation

They are
on vacation.

vacuum cleaner

Here comes the
vacuum cleaner!

van

See Transportation (page 108).

vegetables

He likes vegetables.

very

It is very cold
in there.

vest

See Clothing (page 24).

veterinarian

A veterinarian
helps animals.

village

What a pretty
village!

violin

He is playing
the violin.

visit

He is going to
visit grandma.

volcano

Don't go near
the volcano!

wait

He has to wait
for a bus.

warm

It is warm by
the fire.

wake up

He is about to
wake up.

wash

He washes the
elephant.

wasp

See Insects (page 52).

walk

It is good to
walk.

watch (noun)

Robert is wearing
his new watch.

wall

John is building
a wall.

watch (verb)

Peter likes to
watch ants.

water

The pool is full of water.

we

We are all purple.

weather

What is the weather like today?

Wednesday

On Wednesday, we go to work.

week

Seven days make a week.

welcome

We are always welcome at grandma's house.

well

Thomas builds very well.

well

She doesn't feel well.

west

The sun goes down in the west.

wet

William is wet.

what

What is outside the window?

wheel

The bicycle needs a new wheel.

when

When you sleep, you close your eyes.

where

This is where he keeps his dinner.

which

Which one do you want?

while

I run while he sleeps.

whiskers

This animal has long whiskers.

whisper

This animal needs to whisper.

whistle

They can hear the whistle.

white

See Numbers and Colors (page 68).

who

Who are you?

whole

Can she eat the whole thing?

why

Why is the baby crying?

wife

She is his wife.

wind

The wind is blowing.

window

I can see through the window.

wink

It is fun to wink.

winter

He skis in the winter.

wish

The girl has a wish.

with

The cat is dancing with the dog.

without

He is going without his sister.

woman

My grandma is a
nice woman.

wonderful

They are wonderful
dancers.

woods

Someone is walking
in the woods.

word

Do not say a word.

work (noun)

That is hard work.

work (verb)

She has to work
hard today.

world

The world is
beautiful.

worried

He is worried.

write

Katherine is trying
to write with
the pencil.

wrong

They are
putting on the
wrong hats.

X

X-ray

The X-ray shows his bones.

xylophone

He's a great xylophone player.

Y

yard

There is a dinosaur in our yard!

yawn

What a big yawn!

year

He runs all year.

yellow

See Numbers and Colors (page 68).

yes

Is he yellow? Yes! He is.

yesterday

Yesterday is the day before today.

you

You are reading this book.

your

What color are your eyes?

zebra

You cannot have
a pet zebra!

zipper

The zipper
is stuck.

zero

See Numbers and Colors (page 68).

zoo

I can see
many animals
at the zoo.

zigzag

The house has
zigzags on it.

zoom

Rockets zoom
into space.

zip

The bee wants to
zip her jacket.

A Family Dinner

Dinner is ready! It's time to eat.

Here is your napkin.

The chicken and vegetables look delicious.

Mmmm! They *are* delicious!

Please pass the salt and pepper.

Dinner is great.
Thanks, mom.

You're welcome,
dear.

Do you want
more milk?

No, thank you.

May I please be
excused?

In a few minutes!
But please help us
clear the table, first.

Of course.

Meeting and Greeting

Hello!

Hi!

How are you?

I am fine,
thank you.

What is your name?

My name is Maria.
What is your name?

My name is Susan.

What a beautiful day!

Do you live near the park?

Yes, I live across
the street.

Where do you live?

I live on Main Street.

Do you know what time it is?

It is three o'clock.

Oh, I have to go now.

It was nice to meet you.

Good-bye!

See you soon!

Word List

A

a/an, 7
across, 7
add (to), 7
adventure, 7
afraid (to be), 7
after, 7
again and again, 7
agree (to), 7
air, 7
airplane, 108
airport, 8
all, 8
alligator, 10
almost, 8
along, 8
already, 8
and, 8
answer (to), 8
ant, 52
apartment, 9
apple, 9
April, 9
arm, 76
armadillo, 9
around, 9
art, 9
as, 9
ask (to), 12
at, 12
attic, 86
August, 12
aunt, 12
awake, 12
away, 12

B

baby, 13
back, 13
bad, 13
bag, 13
bakery, 13
ball, 13
balloon, 13
banana, 13
band, 13
bandage, 13

bank, 14
barber, 14
bark (to), 14
baseball, 44
basement, 86
basket, 14
basketball, 44
bat, 14
bat, 14
bathe (to), 14
bathroom, 86
be (to), 14
beach, 15
beans, 15
bear, 10
beautiful, 15
because, 15
bed, 15
bedroom, 86
bee, 52
beetle, 52
before, 15
begin (to), 15
behind, 16
believe (to), 16
bell, 16
belt, 24
berry, 16
best, 16
better, 16
between, 16
bicycle, 108
big, 16
biking, 44
bird, 17
birthday, 17
black, 68
blank, 17
blanket, 17
blouse, 24
blow (to), 17
blue, 68
boat, 108
book, 17
bookstore, 17
boots, 24
bottle, 18
bowl, 18
bowling, 44

box, 18
boy, 18
branch, 18
brave, 18
bread, 18
break (to), 18
breakfast, 18
bridge, 19
bring (to), 19
broom, 19
brother, 19
brown, 68
brush, 19
bubble, 19
bug, 19
build (to), 19
bus, 108
bush, 20
busy, 20
but, 20
butter, 20
butterfly, 52
button, 20
buy (to), 20
by, 20

C

cage, 21
cake, 21
call (to), 21
camel, 21
camera, 21
can, 21
candle, 21
candy, 21
cap, 24
car, 108
card, 22
care (to), 22
carpenter, 22
carrot, 22
carry (to), 22
castanets, 22
castle, 22
cat, 22
caterpillar, 52
catch (to), 23
cave, 23

celebrate (to), 23
chair, 23
chalk, 23
change (to), 23
cheer (to), 23
cheese, 23
cherry, 26
chicken, 10
child, 26
chocolate, 26
circle, 26
circus, 26
city, 26
clap (to), 26
class, 26
classroom, 27
clean, 27
clean (to), 27
climb (to), 27
clock, 27
close, 27
close (to), 27
closet, 86
cloud, 27
clown, 28
coat, 24
cold, 28
comb, 28
comb (to), 28
come (to), 28
computer, 28
cook (to), 28
cookie, 28
count (to), 28
country, 29
cow, 10
crayon, 29
cricket, 52
crowded, 29
cry (to), 29
cup, 29
cut (to), 29
cute, 29

D

dad, 30
dance (to), 30